About the Author

Born and educated in Scotland, Moira Andrew is an ex-teacher and Head Teacher. She was also a lecturer in education at Craigie College of Education, Ayr, and part-time tutor in Creative Writing at the University of Glamorgan. Now a full-time writer and poet-in-schools, Moira has been writing and publishing poetry since the 1980s. Much of her work has been for children and teachers. On the death of her husband, Moira moved from Cardiff to Cornwall. She now lives with her partner in Somerset where she has returned to her first love, writing poetry for adults.

Dedication

For Fiona and Jen,
for Norman,
and in memory of Allen

Moira Andrew

BREAKFAST WITH SWALLOWS

AUSTIN MACAULEY PUBLISHERS™
LONDON • CAMBRIDGE • NEW YORK • SHARJAH

A CIP catalogue record for this title is available from the British Library.

ISBN 978-1-78710-398-6 (Paperback)
ISBN 978-1-78710-399-3 (E-Book)
www.austinmacauley.com

First Published (2017)
Austin Macauley Publishers™ Ltd.
25 Canada Square
Canary Wharf
London
E14 5LQ

Acknowledgments

Some of these poems have been published in 'Reach', (IDP), 'The Dawntreader', (IDP) and 'Sarasvati', (IDP) also by Poetry Space in 'Showcase', in 'Maybe Mabe' and 'Looking Out', (Hovel Press) and in Poetry Cornwall.

PREVIOUS POETRY PUBLICATIONS

Light the Blue Touch Paper, Iron Press; 1986 & 1989
Fresh out of Dragonflies, Headlock; 1995
This Year, Next Year, Marvin Katz Press; 2004 & 2008
Firebird, IDP; 2011
Wish a Wish, (a collection of poetry for children), Poetry Space; 2012
Man in the Moon, IDP; 2014
A Box of Sky, Integral; 2017

BOOKS FOR TEACHERS

Language in Colour, 1989
Words with Wings, 1991
Rainbow Year, 1994
Paint a Poem, 1996
Legend into Language, 1998
Patchwork of Poems, 2000
Tell me a Tale, 2002

Children's poems have appeared in anthologies from OUP, Collins, Scholastic, Macmillan, Ginn etc.
Children's fiction, *Grandad's Party,* Poetry Space, 2016

Contents

Promises, Promises

You promise me
a crocodile
(two turtles
on the side)

In spite of better judgement
I believe you

sort of

A hot day
shadows threading
oak and beech
a lazy river
all rocks and reeds
stitched in sunshine

An unlikely venue
but still I believe you

After all
men make promises
all the time
from *I love you*
downwards

You say
round the next bend
I promise

I imagine
dragon-scales
light-bulb eyes
a snarling smile

Who am I to quibble?
They say all things
(even crocodiles)
are possible

And you haven't let me down

yet

History

My wife, you say, eyeing pork chops
in the pan, *would have a fit
at the amount of oil you use.*
Then, stuffing black bags
for the charity shop,
*We bought this cushion
on our first visit to Egypt ...*
We all have our histories.
You're like Allen, I say,
*He could throw pills
down his throat, just like you.*

Us second-time-rounders
learn to live with the past,
the perfume your wife liked,
my man's taste in shirts,
the duvet cover she bought
at a boot sale, the words
my husband once used,
I shall buy an ounce of silver ...
words you now sing, one man
giving another man back his voice.

The Man with Two Hats

He wore two hats
one on top of the other
and didn't notice
(neither did I, come to that)
went into the kitchen
and forgot why he was there.
He wandered into the bathroom,
the living room, stroked his beard.
I'm worried, he said
I'll forget my own name one day.

But everyone has trouble
remembering dates, phone numbers,
famous poets, jazz-men,
anniversaries. So what?
It's all part of getting older.

I hope it isn't Alzheimer's
he said, holding me close.
*If it is, remember
that I love you.*
A kiss. *Promise?*
I promise, I said.

Just Too Good?

You gave me back
my skin
recharged lips
that had almost forgotten
how to kiss
loaned me
your left shoulder
as a hiding place.

You'd come looking
for me
on the web
when I'd long ago
parcelled you up
under *'a man I'd met
one morning'*
a man who shared
red wine with me
a forest walk
a bath
a bed.

Lying here
swaddled in your arms
as night closes in
I can't believe
how lucky I am.
They say
if something seems
too good to be true
it probably is.

Kilner Jar

I store my words
in glass jars
sometimes they
wink at me like eyes.
I place them on a high shelf
print stick-on labels.
Use before sell-by-date
(but I leave the date open.)

I can never tell
when I'll need them again.
I listen to conversations,
sometimes borrow
other people's spoken words.

My pleasure, he says
not really meaning it
(although it's a nice thought)
so I gather pleasure words
fingertips
   moonstones
      seashore
         anemones
            chocolate
hoard them all
against the cold of winter
like the plums
my mother preserved
in Kilner jars.

I swore they blinked
at me from their shelf
in the kitchen cupboard.
Too much imagination,
that's your trouble!
my mother complained.

Tonight I'll upend a jar
spill words across
the computer screen,
If they gaze wide-eyed at me
I'll wait for them to close,
sleep, dream me a poem.

Keeping Up Appearances

My mother was a firm believer
in standards. *Standards are
very important, girls,* she'd say
smoothing on gloves, finger
by careful finger. She always
wore a hat, even to pop across
to Winnings' Stores for butter.

She was a martyr to bunions
wore narrow bone-crushing shoes
an essential finish to each outfit
always elegant, always discreet
in mole-brown or navy blue.
(Nothing flashy, of course
except on holiday in Cornwall
when she sported a dashing
knee-length split skirt with style.)

She preened herself in the role
of Mrs Brown, the dentist's wife
at her best posing on art-deco chairs
in Cranston's' tea-rooms, waitresses
in black satin frocks with white cuffs.

My mother disliked any show
of emotion. Kissing in the street
or walking hand-in-hand were no-nos
Not very nice, she'd say. Sometimes
I think about what she missed –
hair falling free across her eyes
spontaneous kisses, raw sex, (neither
trusted nor talked about.) As for my dad,
I reckon he probably lost out too.

Sweetshop

Sometimes
I hoard words
like boiled sweets
in fat glass jars
on the shelves
of the Misses Hutchinson's
corner shop
where we hurried
after school.

Occasionally
I keep a few
extra-specials
in silver paper
blue, purple, lipstick-red
(the Quality Street
of words)
for extra-special poems
like the top-end chocolates
the ladies tipped out
on the counter
if they happened to feel
in a benign mood
and their bunions
weren't playing up.

Now and again
words work
and come together
in screwed-up
paper bags
like a sweet treat
we used to suck
in the tram
on the way home.

Disappointment

I've always been a terrible trial
to my mother, never lived up
to her high expectations.

Christmas morning, *Mummy,* I shout,
Look what Santa's brought! My parents
are awake, expecting excitement.

After all, they've saved up to buy
a doll-sized Marmet pram, pale blue,
a replica of the real thing.

In my hands, a string of coloured
beads, glittering red, green, gold
as they catch the winter light.

Probably costing half-a-crown,
probably from Woolworths, the
highlight of my Christmas.

Of course, I'd disappointed
my mother from the start – she
told me she'd hoped for a boy.

Triggers

Anything that starts a train of thought ....

waiting in a dark place
for that first shudder
of sunlight
      like searching
      for the warmth
      of a shoulder to lean on
stroking the fine-china petals
of an early snowdrop
beneath the hedge
      like the unexpected joy
      of foot on naked foot
living with
the woody smell
from underground spaces
      like breathing
      the musk of after-sex
trampling on fairy rings
as a blackbird takes to the air

its pure yellow song a banner
      like a long-silenced voice
      re-invented
      in another man's music

... and moves thought to action

Breakfast with Swallows

Black wizards on the wing
skiing the slopes of air
landing with precision
on the washing line
voices replete with song
they pause, titivate, nibbling
at pale under-feathers
one careful wing at a time
remember the partner
on the nest, visit briefly
bearing a beakful
of thread-fine insects.

They pirouette, showing off
their skills as trapeze artists
completely ignoring us
sitting in the morning sun
a striped umbrella shading
the bowl of fresh fruit
our coffee and toast.
We chat in the fractured
fashion of familiarity. Above us
the birds chatter too, allowing us
to share their music
their yellow mountain air.

Cyprus in the Rain

It's a day to make soup
build shelves
cut logs for the fire
put a bucket in place
to catch water
pouring through the roof.
It's a day when hilltops
merge into spit-grey cloud
streets run like rivers in spate
and puddles draw circles
on the patio tiles.
It's a day to try your hand
at drop-scones – gone in a flash
hot from the pan.
Hard to remember
yesterday when we sat
under Colin's vine drinking coffee
and putting the world to rights
the sky kitchen-tablecloth blue
hills etched in fine-nib ink
every detail of rock, every cleft
Leonardo-clear. Perhaps
today is the perfect day
to go to bed and make love?

Goose Feathers

Not the wall-to-wall yellow
we'd been led to expect
the sky goose-feather grey
laden with the weight
of an unspent sun lolling
back against the hills,
the air thick, humid, heavy.

Trees and bushes, leaves
brittle, ash-grey in sympathy
stand parched, sun-scorched,
exhausted and breathless,
an occasional bougainvillaea
the only blink of colour
in a goose-grey landscape.

The mountains, summits
haunted by ash-grey cloud,
mourn blackened brushwood
ravaged by summer fires.
A cinder-black tree stands guard,
bleak as graffiti scrawled
on a newly-painted wall.

Geese in their v-flight
having long-since escaped
to cooler summer skies
leave us to grey Syrian
sand-storms goose-stepping
across mountain tops, feathers
falling grey on grey.

Big Summer

The garage man shrugs,
glares at the yellow sky,
Big summer, he says
by way of explanation.
Heat leans cracked elbows
on hilltops, red-tiled roofs
      and hatless heads,
            laughs aloud.

The sun breathes
dragon-fire, furnace-
hot, cruel. Flowers
wilt, melons bleed juice,
and figs fall fat from
the trees. Fun and games
      to the beast roaring
        across the sky.

A burst of flame sets
the mountain-side alight
swallowing brushwood,
olives and prickly pear.
Blackened bare-boned trees
stand sentinel by the road.
      The joker in the sky smiles,
         almost satisfied.

We sweat, shower, sink
down on the bed to rest.
Too hot for clothes, too
hot for sex, we link
fingers, switch on the fan,
lie separate, motionless,
      to a cackle of laughter
         from the heavens.

In the cool of the evening
we have the last laugh,
tall brandy sours,
candle glittering, bread
and olives, cheese and wine,
jollity from the taverna below.
      Big summer, subdued,
         till dawn flicks its switch.

Deep Pockets

The mountains
have dark pockets
hide whole villages
in their depths,
roofs tucked together
like crumpled receipts,
the cracked church bells
a bunch of keys
lost in the lining.

Come night,
hills and mountains
shrug off purple shirts,
hang trousers
upside-down
on a sky-hook,
snuggle naked
into the moon's
waiting arms.

Trouser pockets
empty their hoard –
the busy café,
a pond alive
with sex-hungry frogs,
shadowed hugger-
mugger houses,
their lighted windows
sparkling
like loose change.

Portrait of a Bearded Man

I hear him in the dark silence
of a Cyprus night, when
the candle has guttered
to a stub, bickering cicadas
have called a truce, after taverna
tables have been stored inside.
> *I hear him in the opening bars*
> *of 'Bye Bye Blackbird'*

I see him in the moon hanging
crooked on its silver hook, in the
church tower with its one-tongued bell,
in the yellow-ochre, burnt-sienna of rock
as we drive the scrotum-tightening
(he says) vertiginous mountain roads.
> *I see him in the shirtless man*
> *sun-worshipping on the patio.*

I smell him in the hot fat of Lukamades
the woman in a wrap-round apron
spooning Sunday treats into honeyed
vanilla water, in the black olives
on a market stall, in pork cooking
on an open fire, in newly-baked bread.
> *I smell him in the garlicky breath*
> *cheftalia leaves behind.*

I taste him in the gold bars
of sunshine, in the salt of our sweat
as we lie on top of the bed, barely
touching, skin leaking on skin, in
the tall brandy sours he makes
on the dot of six every evening.
> *I taste him in the fingertips*
> *slid between my lips.*

I feel him in the thick Cyprus heat
as we arrive in the wrong clothes
at Paphos late in the evening, under
the cool wave of air-conditioning
in the bedroom, in the roughness
of a peach, the juice of a melon.
> *I feel him in the prickle of beard*
> *as we kiss and kiss good-night.*

Pre-Packaged

crouched foetus-like
        snug
in its brown paper parcel
made to fit a man's hand
        a flower waits
day after winter's day
        listening
to the tick of a green clock
itching to unfurl its gaudy
        yellowness
                into the cool blue air
of an April morning

Another April
(For Allen)

It's the blackbirds' fault – again!
They sit there, all bursting lungs
and exuberance, drilling holes in
the early evening air – a ruse
       to emphasise loneliness.

To be exact, it's the whole spring
thing that brings it back, bluebells
fingering the grass, an anodised sea,
clematis making pale pink thumb-
       prints on the fence.

The sheer over-the-topness of
exploding colour, the cockiness
of every male bird in the region
and impatient prepubescent leaves
       must share the blame.

They conspire to conjure up
the last slow days of your life,
nothing but Iraq on the telly, your
breathlessness, the acid-yellow
       unrelenting sunshine.

I write my poems, drink my wine
and try not to cry, but anger eats
me from the outside in as another
guiltless April unwinds its beauty to
        an unappreciative audience.

Obsession

Like the man
before him
he tolerates
my love affair
even buys a bunch
for the kitchen table
the feisty smell
in-your-face colour
a breakfast wake-up.

Not for me a single bunch
I stand flowers
all over the house
jugs, bowls, glass vases
and the garden
brims over
with yellowness
pots on the patio
bulbs in the grass.

The daffodil man
on the pier
has my order ready
£4's worth
fat buds still green
with promise
my guy shakes his head
Positively obsessed!
he says smiling.

'All Day It Has Rained'

The garden licks cracked dry lips – at
the first teasing drop, it lies limp, open-limbed
      in glorious surrender.

In tubs and pots, flowers shudder with
pent-up desire, eyes closed, as they gulp down
      every last warm drop.

Colours spiral out of control, for gold
read grey, for yellow, gunmetal – green multiplies,
      deepens to almost-black.

Unremembered sounds – a whisper in the grass,
a shushing of high-hat brushes, the surge and spit
      of overwhelmed drains.

In forgotten colours, in stripes and dots,
flushed umbrellas bloom, monstrous mushrooms
      thrusting into liquid air.

Tongue slack, lips swollen, the garden relaxes
under a watery sun, in the heady aftermath
      of wanton indulgence.

Anemones

I saw them in the rain,
in Clevedon, between
the wine shop and
the bakers, a bucketful
of curled and crippled buds,
wrapped in paper.

Done up in tens,
they were, all colour
hidden. *I'll take two,*
I said and grey stems
leaked their milk
down my coat.

A day of indoor heat
unlocked the buds
and such purples,
such blues and reds
escaped to frame their
soot-thumbed eyes.

I loved their grace
stooping in the glass,
tried to capture it
in paint, flat on paper –
like sticking pins
into butterflies.

Summer Sea, Gyllyngvase

Along the path, giddy wild geraniums jive,
petals a fierce in-your-face indigo – beside such
true blueness, the sea fades to silver-birch grey.

The sun, no more than a misted mirror, is held
tight in the arms of jade-green fields, rich yachts
dwindle to mere thumb-prints on the horizon.

Mermaids, tired of their own voices, are invisible
to the naked eye, the only clue, a jewel-dazzle
of scales as they hitch a ride on incoming waves.

Dead Tree

a brutal statement
        alabaster lightning bolts
                against a slab of orange

the savagely knotted design
        skinned and flayed
                defiant in its nakedness

exposed to the four winds
        like the Angel of the North
                a perch for predatory birds

ringed by younger cousins
        greening up for spring
                the tree rears its gaunt head

contempt in every limb
        its knot-holed arrogance
                staring death in the eye

Winter Twilight

for a moment
little more
than a nano-second
white-rose shadow
outlines each branch
every wishbone twig
with the delicacy
of a fine Chinese brush
and the sun spreads
a wash of coltsfoot yellow
along the hedge-tops
swamped
in the blink of an eye
by streamers of scarlet
in a last rush of colour
across the evening sky
before the paint-box
closes its lid
for the night

Yellow Tulips

I wonder, you say,
how they manage to grow
so many tulips all the same?
I look at their cupped yellow
hands, more interested
in their colour, like
borrowed sunshine, than
the logistics of growing them –
identical twins, triplets, quads.

I finger the smooth finish,
relish their elegance,
their sheer sensuality – at
£2.50 for eight it's a bargain
for my five-day love-in.
They only get one flower
from each bulb in a season,
you go on, trying to assess
their business viability.

Tulips die with gentleness
opening in slow motion
to butterfly wings, each petal
falling soft as a naked footfall.
I wonder how it's worth
their while to grow vast fields
of one-off flowers ... Two
different takes on one bunch
of tulips from Sainsbury's.

Jazz Hands

Making music in the night
those black winter trees
Satchmos of the forest
coax rich jazz notes
          from the wind.

A flock of sleek crows
writes sheet music
on leafless branches
crotchets and minims
          all in Bb.

Snow falls, five-finger twigs
wearing white gloves
jazz hands of the thirties,
draw rhythm and blues
          from the cold air.

The woods come alive
with sound, trumpet, bass,
trombone, soaring clarinet
tempting a new moon to jive
          among the stars.

Jazz on a Sunday Afternoon
(For Pee Wee Ellis)

the fat black man
(dark shirt, dark suit)
smiles a fat contented smile
fondles his saxophone
brass keys smouldering
in autumn sunlight
fat fingers exploring
a silent melody
in anticipation

a tentative breath
nod to the pianist
and he's away
a painter loading his brush
with mahogany colours
(browns sepias russets)
spreading glory
in great splashes of sound
across the October afternoon

And the Band Played On

Sunshine, a wide lawn
tea cups, wine glasses
on tables, an audience
stretched out on the grass.

The band launches into
Ice-cream, their opening
number, trumpet, trombone
banjo, keyboard, clarinet ...

Applause, the first drops
A shower, they murmur
unearthing coats, unfurling
umbrellas. Some pack up.

Others sit tight under trees.
A thunderflash, a deluge.
The audience evaporates,
just wives in rainhoods left.

The band, enjoying its music-
making, plays *Birth of the Blues*
and two small girls, one in yellow
one in pink take centre stage.

They keep in perfect rhythm,
dancing on wet grass, twirl
pirouette, hair drenched, dresses
soaked, alive only to the beat.

Flattered, the band plays on.

Fairy Dust

Sunday night, a jazz jam
in the Corner House pub.
A couple arrive, with
their 16-year-old son,
a saxophonist, in tow.

We move up to make
room. Among our
trousers and tops
the woman is an exotic,
bright pink tights,

matching flower
in her hair, a skirt
made from layer upon
layer of net – it should've
given me a clue.

She takes out her knitting,
An obsessive, her husband
confides. *I wish I'd brought
my glasses,* she says,
fingers working furiously.

The young man is invited
to sit in. Like the band, the
needles reach a crescendo.
That's my boy! the woman says,
eyes glazed with pride.

She puts the knitting down
long enough to applaud
her son's solo. Despite
the din, I hear her say
she'd worked till half past six.

Conversation isn't easy.
So what do you do? I ask.
I'm a fairy, she says.
I make fairy dust. I sink back
on the sofa, wine in hand.

Christmas Apples

Her words sent a surge of dread
rippling up my spine, I remember.
She was ready to go home, coat on,
car keys in hand, strands of tinsel
draped across her arm. The afternoon
was winter-dark. *'Another Christmas
over and done with,* she said.
One nearer the grave for all of us.

I stopped what I was doing
and stared at her. She was right,
of course, but I didn't want to think
about our mortality. Nobody does.
I returned the Christmas apples
to their boxes for another year,
loving their roundness, wrapping
each smooth shell in tissue paper.

It had been busy. A school Christmas
always is, late nights, angel outfits,
tinsel haloes, shepherds in tea-towels,
small children panda-eyed with
excitement, exhaustion. But, come
the start of the holidays, decorations
must be taken down, leaving a clean
sweep for New Year's back-to-basics.

Strange how it happens – after
a decade of daily contact, she
had all but slipped my mind,
down to an annual greetings card
with the familiar signature, *Joyce & Tom.*
This year had been no different.
Except for the funeral, that is, when
for her, Christmas was finally over.

Broken Child

She looks up at me, concentrates,
grasps a pen in cold fingers … like
a key it opens doors in the sky
and stars fall, silver, into her lap.

She pauses, listens, and a blackbird
lends her his music … she showers
in tumbling waterfalls … and
the needle in the back of her hand

shrinks to a pinprick. She smiles,
her bed is a boat, the beeping
monitor a grandmother clock, an
assiduous drip the Man-in-the-Moon.

She draws a rainbow in fluorescent
felt-tips … lies back on her pillow,
protective hand over her poem,
sleeps to the silence of snowflakes.

No Rehearsal

You think you're psyched up
ready for everything
life can throw at you –
until the worst happens.

You pick yourself up, phone
family, friends, neighbours.
You sound together, after all
you've been anticipating it.

The reality's nothing like
your best-laid schemes, tears
threaten, a wobble in the voice.
I know. I've been there.

It's our neighbour's turn
today. I expect she's picked up
his cast-off shirt, emptied his
pockets, hung up his keys.

I imagine the bed still smells
of him, a half-eaten sandwich
loiters in the fridge. She tries
on her widow's face for size.

Max's flag flies at half-mast.

The Fixer

He's the go-to man –
a jar of olives
an ounce of cornflour
a three-pin adaptor.
He'll even acquire
a bargain-price
double bed and install it
complete with duvet.
Tall, gentle of smile
quiet of voice
he stoops at the neck
like some upmarket
Hampstead street-lamp.
He lives alone
with his boats
hand-crafted tables
inherited cook-books
keeps *The Chronicle* alive
in memory of his wife –
her death, the only thing
he couldn't fix.

A Nice Cup of Tea

They tell me
I make a good cup of tea –
not that I'd know
I don't drink the stuff,
can't stand the smell,
astringent, sour, thoroughly
unappetising.

I've brewed tea
first thing in the morning
for the men in my life –
and for my daughter,
a compulsive tea-Jenny
(well-named) She takes it
milky, by the bucketful.

I remember making tea
for my mother, bringing it
to her bedside, she in curlers
and blue hairnet. She struggled
to sit up, *Thanks dear,* she said,
not knowing. I had to tell her,
Mum ... Dad died in the night.

Blackbird Bye-Bye

Every time we drive
along London Road
on the way into Bath,
I think blackbirds
baby blackbirds
to be precise,
all open beaks
yolk-yellow throats.

From a basement flat
no garden, no green
we climbed up steps
to a grey street
forgettable pavements
blank black windows
a hum of traffic
from the road below.

Conversation flowed,
stopped – in lieu of trees
an enterprising family
had commandeered
a lamp-post, nest buttonholed
into a narrow crack –
seven eager heads
swivelling to greet us.

We left them waiting
for assiduous parents
to swoop in with hard-won
titbits – where from?
we wondered. *I expect
we'll write about this
one day,* we promised.
I left it too late to ask

if you'd got around to it.

Three Roses

We bought flowers in M&S
(it was her birthday) yellow roses
although she'd have preferred
white. I arranged three
in a green beer bottle
placed them on her grave.

It's the kind of thing we do
we who are left, in memory
(as if we'd forget.) I usually light
a candle for my man's birthday
put it in the garden beside
his Welsh poppies.

Not that either of them
is any the wiser, beyond
caring about roses or candles.
As a child I imagined dead people
crowded shoulder to shoulder
on a cloud somewhere.

I wondered why they didn't
fall off, thinking there must be
a cloud-shortage by now.
Still do. We left the flowers
shining like little suns, held hands
walked into a new yellow day.

In Memoriam

You wonder
what you'll leave
behind. A garden?
I've created two
from scratch
one altered
beyond recognition,
the other now
a wilderness, so
a next-door neighbour
tells me. Poems?
I've written dozens
lots published
but who reads them?

My daughter says
she thinks of me
when she smells
ironing – a smell
that's on its own,
pungent, sharp
not quite burning.
It's the one household task
I enjoy – the smoothing
the folding, the placing
in a drawer ready
for next time round.

Each time my daughter
irons her tee-shirts
(once a week or so)
she'll remember me,
better a smell than
Beloved Mother
inscribed
on a headstone

Red Umbrellas
(For Di)

sadness
seeps from winter clouds
in fine silver-grey ribbons
flutters
across my eyes
and sharp knots of sorrow
finger my heart

language
no longer works
words like metastasis
grow legs
jump out of locked boxes
kicking and screaming
as we stand helpless
and soaked to the skin

none of us
can know how it feels
we can only wait
beside you
in the rain
bright red umbrellas up
sheltering you
from the worst
of the storm

Dark by the End

I expect it's the same
for all of us – dark
by the end, dark like
under a stone
dark like somewhere
behind the moon,
dark as a night-rose.

My man died
in bright sunlight,
just after mid-day
one April afternoon,
his cousin
in the street, fresh
from a business lunch.

Black holes come
to mind – or do we step
along a narrow path
footfall by footfall
under overhanging trees
to the end of the line
where inevitably

the dark is waiting?

White Nightdress

Think of a nightdress
an old-fashioned
white cotton nightdress
buttoned-up, lace
at the neck.

My grandmother
wrapped hers
in tissue paper, stored
it in a drawer, ready
for the inevitable.

Of course, when
she finally needed
the nightdress, she
was no longer around
to appreciate it.

Think of the child
peering round the door,
her grandmother
lying still and cold
under a pink quilt.

*Gran looks like she's
sleeping,* they'd told her.
They lied. Grandmother
was nothing like herself
asleep or awake.

Worst of all, a wisp
of cotton wool escaped
from her lips. Think of
the child longing, but not
daring, to tuck it in.

Emptiness

The chair opposite
is empty,
no cat locked
beneath your left arm,
no half-full glass
of red wine
on the bookcase
by your side,
no muttered comments
on the rolling news.

Your grey eyes
no longer share
a smile with me,
the Guardian
is smooth, unwrinkled
until I open it, starting
as I always do
at the first page –
not you – you
work back to front.

That vacant chair,
is yours, yours alone.
The cat ignores it.
I sit opposite,
book in my lap,
glass within reach –
the sinister palm tree
stares in,
and the clock ticks
in an empty room.

Portrait of Mary

(Queen Mother and Child with Pheasant
by Kate Lynch)

She's tired of posing,
tired of her celebrity status
of sitting upright
in yet another blue outfit
with that half-smile
wavering around her lips.

And she's pretty fed up
with the Christ-child
showing off like mad,
sucking up to his teachers.
Why not a proper boy –
scowls, tantrums, skinned knees?

Tarnished crown tilted
to one side, she hugs
a live bird, bright feathers
flaming across her breast.
Eyes half-closed, she shies
away from wringing its neck.

The boy, moon-faced, six
or so, leans against
his mother's left shoulder.
He wears clean blue jeans
a red top. Bored to bits, they
sit waiting for things to happen.

Fine Art

at eye-level
flowers have eternal life
their reds red
petals crisp unfallen
calyx open-mouthed
butter-yellow

the jug is fat
blue-spotted
forever filled with water
and in the distance
the sea is a wash
of blue-bag blue

nothing moves
nothing smells
no sound no decay
like a photograph
of dead people
where everyone's smiling
and showing their teeth

In This Woman's Mind

This woman
half-asleep
paints pictures
      in her mind.

She paints
in lurid reds,
in yellows
      fierce as daffodils.

She dreams
of love-making,
of closeness
      to a man's body.

In her head
she tries to write
but her words
      won't play ball.

She wakes
shivering, reaches
for the man
      asleep beside her.

She kisses
the man, painting
his whiskery lips
      in vivid red.

This woman finds
her lost words, writes
a poem, yellow with
love and daffodils.

Fog in the Forecast

Extensive hill-fog developing
the weather-man says –
I know all about that
these days – the television's
feathery edges, blurred
mid-vision. *Hello Simon,* I say
when the window-cleaners
call. *It's Adrian,* he says.
I apologise, *Sorry, hard*
to tell the difference
under these woolly caps,
but really it's the fog
developing in my eyes.

Even in my dreams
faces are fog-bound
I don't immediately
recognise my husband
sitting in a corner
emaciated and without
his glasses, *You're back,*
I say, *Not before time.*
I bend down to peer
at him, *Can I kiss you?*
He reaches out. I drift
into his arms and my dodgy
eyes no longer matter.

Food for the Eyes

I gobble down green,
new-born leaves, grass,
hedgerows, lily-pads,
swallowing colour whole
its exuberance
its glorious extravagance
exciting blurred
winter-starved taste buds
in my pepper-pot eyes.

Hard to take in
the over-the-top abundance
of green against blue.

I store surplus greenness,
and outrageous colour
in screw-top jars
against the day
when dancing patterns
of sun and shade
in leaf-laden lanes
lose their flavour,
leaving their succulence

to dry on my tongue,
the taste of green
melting into memory.

The Wind and the Sun

A man you once slept with
blusters online, puffing out
his cheeks like the east wind,
remembering. *Stunning!* he writes
describing the encounter
in embarrassing detail.
I've never forgotten it.

You hadn't given it a thought
from that day to this.
Too much sun, too much wine,
a tumble in the hay-loft –
just one of those things
from a long time ago
and you've moved on.

He first flatters – to no effect,
tries bully-boy tactics
attempting to blow off top
and trousers in one fell swoop
as a show of strength.
*I should've taken you to bed
when I had the chance!*

(Taken? He's got the wrong
woman – not likely!) You
clutch your jumper ever more
tightly around you. *Thanks,*
you email back, *but it's
dead-as-a-doorknob history.
I'm spoken for. Forget it!*

Instant reply. *What's he got?*
He's in storm-warning mode
so you let him into the secret.
The other man smiled,
gentled you, like the sun
in summer and your clothes
fell to the floor one by one.

Forbidden Fruit

The woman stands naked
but for a scarlet sunhat.
She wriggles her toes
in the warm earth, stretches
sun-baked arms, sighs.

A fine-tuned breeze fingers
the fruit trees, tickles
their brittle leaves, sun
touching up the orchard
with hot searching hands.

The man can't believe
his luck. He loiters in
the shadows, watching,
waiting. The woman reaches
for a low-hanging branch.

Breasts taut, nipples proud
she selects an apple, twists
it from its twig. She cups
its weight in her hand, pulls
down the brim of her hat.

She sits, takes a first bite.
The man makes his move,
steps into the sunlight, folds
the woman in his arms, kisses
her, tasting the sweet juice.

Forgotten, the apple falls
to the ground. It's true,
the man thinks, *Red hat, no
knickers.* A worm squirms
from the apple's white core.

Reality Check

I lost an earring in Amsterdam,
one minute there it was
silver in the sun
then gone
taking the shine off canals
tulips, coffee shops.

I mourned its loss
after all, the globes
were a present
one of the first from you
just perfect, like little lights
switched on
by every movement.

Never mind, you said.
*Can't be helped – was that
one we found under the duvet
once before?* No such luck
this time. I needed a kiss.

The following day's headline
complete with photograph
orange jumpsuit
raised silver blade
put the lost earring
into perspective.

Dying to Live

Bodies on top of me,
some twitching, I waited
for the bullet ... She goes
quiet. *I wondered what*
it would be like to die.

She tells of blood dripping
into her eyes, down her legs.
I tried desperately not to move.
She can't go on. *In my head*
I said good-bye to my mum.

Out for the evening, music,
wine, kisses – another world.
My boyfriend. Where is he?
she frets. *I haven't seen*
him since Friday night.

The slow-flowing Seine,
glittering lights, the Eiffel
Tower, the Paris we know
and love. This girl is one
of many, her story unique.

We grieve for her, for
the guys at the bar,
the soccer fans. We can
only wait and watch, all dying
to live for one more day.

The Sky at Night

A sky
frantic with stars
fills
its shadows
with the sadness
of owl-cries
of scurrying creatures
of dark dreams
where the man
at your side
calls out
What's going on?
and there's no way
you can answer
so you hold out
both hands
trying
to catch a falling star
a gift
a talisman
just for him
before it melts
leaving only
tu-wit-to-woo's
leaking through
your cold fingers.

Love in Socks

A man once tried
to make love to me.
He was young
sexy with floppy hair.
He said *I love you.*
I fancied him like mad.

He was married.
I was married, but
that didn't stop us.
We kissed, kissed
again, laughed, threw
clothes on the floor.

We trailed fingers
along arms, down legs,
skin against skin.
I looked down – he
still wore black socks.
That was it. No way

could I make love
to a man in socks.
I squeezed out of bed,
dressed, drove home,
his voice in my ears,
What did I do wrong?

Going Up

They'd said their good-byes
it was never going to work
       that much was obvious.

She was rushed, sweaty-hot, glanced
at her watch, snatched at the doors
       as they slid shut.

They re-opened, as if by magic,
his big-bear presence filling the space,
       emptying it of air.

He reached for the Level 10 button,
gathered her into his arms. She leaned
       against his bulk.

They didn't kiss, simply absorbed
one another, the atmosphere fizzing
       with damped-down sex.

By Ground Level it was over, he fielded
his briefcase, she pressed the up button,
       made it to her meeting on time.

Brief Encounters

Laurie Lee once kissed me,
but then, he kissed lots of women –
he loved them – from Rosie onwards.

And I danced with Russell Hoban,
a short man in a wide-brimmed hat,
who half-heartedly propositioned me.

I had supper with Ted Hughes in
a farmhouse kitchen, sat at his feet
as he read poems, his voice sexy, deep.

They talk about these dead writers
on Radio 4. Our lives once collided,
(not that they'd have remembered)

but it's a brief claim to fame. Then there
are the poets I've worked with, still
about, still broadcasting, still writing.

In the past, I've slept with a poet or two,
their names long-forgotten, but nothing

        absolutely nothing,
matches that one kiss from Laurie Lee.

Donkey Lane

They say nobody walks
for the sake of walking
these days. Not so.
Early afternoon, blue sky
clear air, brook rushing
towards the river. We zip up
coats, pull on hat and
gloves, *Which way?*

                We go
past the pub, the church,
past the churned-up stream
where ducks ride the flow,
turn along Donkey Lane.
Birds are giddy with today's
hint of spring, check out last
year's nest-sites.

              We find
a smattering of snowdrops
by the bridge, a solitary daffodil
testing the air, oaks still sketched
in winter's pen-and-ink.

                    We meet
dog-walkers, hikers,
strollers, couples hand-
in-hand. *Hi,* we exchange
in casual greeting. A young
woman stops, *Mr Leater?*
He used to be my tutor,
she tells her man.
                    We talk
in the shorthand of everyday,
make for home, by-passing
the castle, pat pockets
for keys, open up, switch
on the kettle.

After the Hottest Day

Sometimes a ready meal
fills the bill, like tonight
sitting under a sun umbrella
in the cool of the evening
chores behind us –
pots watered,
filing, emails dealt with,
washing ironed, fresh
from the line, fruit in the fridge
ready for tomorrow's breakfast –
now it's wine-time
fountain burbling, Ottilie Patterson
singing *There'll be a hot time
in the old town tonight,* cold
white wine reaching my ankles,
an M&S microwave meal, raspberries
cream, a scatterbrain breeze
troubling the trees. He takes
my hand, squeezes it, says
'I'll bring things out,' sets our meal
on the garden table. Geraniums
nod, share their true-blueness
their smattering of perfume.
He looks around, remembering,
'This patio's always been underused.
She wasn't up to it.' Like Ottilie,
I can't give him anything but love.

Cocoa and Crumpets

Fuelled by adrenaline
after a successful gig
you can't sleep, yawn, turn,
toss. Sex doesn't work.
We are mesmerised by
the shipping forecast,
shift back to back. Sleep
remains a world away.

Give up? you say, flicking
on the bedside light. We
pull on dressing gowns,
stumble into the kitchen,
pop crumpets in the toaster
Butter melts, puddles
yellow over white plates.
I make cocoa, you Horlicks.

We talk, hold hands,
unpick the gig. *I forgot*
to sing the last verse of
Careless Love, you say.
Did you notice? I didn't.
Posh candle-lit suppers
are all very well - sometimes
hot crumpets hit the spot.

Conversations

When fingers do the talking
they tell it like it is
no jokes, no one-up-manship
they don't try to be clever.
Fingers are pragmatists
make contact, skin to skin
trace bumps and cracks
hills and plains, mapping
the foreign territory
of another's body.
They make no comment
on their discoveries, simply
take every new sensation
as it comes, storing each touch
like buried treasure
at the very furthest tip
where nail meets print.
Fingers don't need reassurance
don't ever have to ask *Is this real?*
They already know the answer.

A Box of Sky

the sky is a box,
a box of secrets
its lid tilted, half-open
trinkets, love-words
broken beads
spilling out
on the world below

the box is round,
part washed-out pink
part a clear blue
merging into amethyst
clouds feathering
the shattered lock, like
a design in slip-wear

and always, always
secrets, rows of XXXs
on faded letters
on lovers' lips
on the softest skin
where thighs
meet body parts

a brisk wind
tears at the hinge
lid spiralling downwards
every last secret
tumbling to catch
on treetops, on rooftops
the sky ripped open –

just another empty box

Clay Pots

It is not the business
of the gods
to bake clay pots ...

They stand,
row upon row
rounded pink
open-mouthed
dreaming of
trailing begonias
geraniums
olive trees
in yellow sunlight.

We wait
row upon row
of schoolgirls
in navy skirts
striped ties
dreaming of
boys, of nearly-men
our pink mouths
ripe for kisses.

When the time
is right, we
and they will flower, pots
overflow with blossom
scattered pink petals,
we with promises
of undying love
our bellies billowing
with unborn babies.